Psychopaths and Love

ADELYN BIRCH

© 2015 ADELYN BIRCH

All rights reserved. No parts of this publication may be reproduced, stored in a retrieval system, or transmitted, in any form or by any means, electronic, mechanical, photocopying, recording, or otherwise, without the prior permission of the author.

CONTENTS

INTRODUCTION — vi

1 What is a Psychopath? — 1

2 The Mask of the Psychopath…and What Lies Beneath — 8

3 Psychopath as Gigolo — 14

4 Psychopath as Charmer — 18

5 Red Flags of a Psychopath — 22

6 Stages of the Psychopathic Bond — 29

7 Emotional Rape — 34

8 Covert Emotional Manipulation — 37

9 The Game You Didn't Know You Were Playing — 45

10 Intensity or Intimacy? — 49

11 Know What You Want and Need — 54

12 Faith That You Will Heal is the Key to Healing — 58

13	Healing in the Aftermath	61
14	Your Own Personal Apocalypse	66
15	Traits of the Psychopath's Victim	70
16	The Self-compassion Effect	76
17	Feelings of loss and grief after the psychopath is gone?	82
18	How to Help a Friend Who Was Victimized by a Psychopath	85
19	Freedom from the Psychopath	91
	About the Author	93

INTRODUCTION

You fell down the rabbit hole.

You didn't know it—you only thought you had found true love. You left the mundane world behind and didn't look back, nor did you want to. It never crossed your mind to question the things too good to be true, the things beyond imagination, the strange things. Why would you? After all, they didn't seem so strange on that side of the looking glass.

In that world of awe, you didn't ask too many questions. But then white magic turned to black, and it was too late. You had been hooked, deceived and taken for a ride.

My hope for you is that this book will give you not just information, but also help you feel understood and let you know you're not alone. This is so important and yet so often lacking for those of us who find ourselves victimized in this way. That shouldn't be, because it happens more often and to more people than anyone would guess. Most people, myself included, didn't even know anything like this was possible.

Believe that you will heal, and know that there is life and love after this.

If you have not yet been victimized by a psychopath, I hope this book will help you gain knowledge and awareness that will enable you to avoid that fate.

Best wishes to you on your journey.

1

WHAT IS A PSYCHOPATH?

Psychopaths are social predators, both male and female, who do not have a conscience or the ability to feel love, compassion, fear or remorse. It is believed that psychopathy is a genetic neurobiological disorder.

Evolutionary psychology offers an alternate theory that psychopathy is not a disorder, but an evolutionary adaptation. This theory views psychopathy as a social strategy, one that benefits the individual instead of the group.

Whatever the cause, psychopathy creates individuals who share certain characteristics that differ greatly from the norm.

"Psychopathy refers to a pathological personality disposition that involves charm, manipulation, and ruthless exploitation of others. Psychopathic persons are lacking in conscience and feeling for others; they selfishly take what they want and do as they please without the slightest sense of guilt or regret." (Hare, Neumann, & Widiger, 2012)

The psychopath considers life a game to be played and "won" at the expense of others. Inflicting harm, whether it be psychological, spiritual, physical or financial, is acceptable to them.

Self-gratification is the only thing that motivates them and all that they live for.

Psychopaths play their game primarily to fulfill their insatiable desires for power and control. They also play to meet their secondary needs for things like sex, money, prestige, or the illusion of a marriage that furthers their goals in some way. Psychopaths often derive pleasure from their victim's suffering, because it makes them feel superior. While this is incomprehensible to normal humans, it's just life as usual for the psychopath.

Psychopaths are pathological liars who will say anything to get what they want.

With traits like these, you'd never expect a psychopath to be charming, but they are often extraordinarily so.

Psychopaths wear what's called "the mask of sanity," which hides the truth that lies beneath. The Mask allows them to move through society undetected. They're smooth talkers with a lot to say. They're totally relaxed since they have no fear or anxiety, and this makes others around them relax. Strong social skills and unshakable confidence are their predatory edge; these skills bring the psychopath into contact with many potential victims, and make these "targets" comfortable and open to contact.

Just when you need your intuition to alert you to danger, it will be disarmed by the psychopath.

Psychopaths and love are an impossible combination. They aren't able to experience love, and they consider it a weakness that creates vulnerability that they can use to their advantage. These predators gain a victim's trust and love and then involve them in devastating sham relationships that inevitably result in serious harm.

Psychopaths feel contempt for normal human emotions. We show our humanness in the form of love, insecurity, fear, remorse, trust and anxiety, and they consider these emotions unforgivable weaknesses, vulnerabilities that make us easy targets for manipulation, and deserving of it!

Victims are manipulated into trying to suppress any display of the emotions that disgust the psychopath, but that's not possible, especially since they provoke them at the same time. They will leak out one way or another, igniting the psychopath's contempt. In other words, there is no way to establish an intimate relationship with a psychopath. He will despise you, guaranteed... but keep using you anyway as long as you have something he wants or until he finds a fresh victim to fulfill his needs.

Psychopaths often establish a relationship with a target based on a hidden agenda from day one, the only goal being victimization. They are human predators who completely hide their real identities and create a tailor-made persona to gain the trust and love of their victim so they can dominate, control and manipulate them. Self-gratification is what drives them.

Sometimes they may pursue a relationship without an explicit intent to victimize and harm. They may become "fascinated" with someone because of their beauty or intelligence, or the belief that they've met their "equal." This doesn't change the fact that psychopaths end up hurting the people they get close to, and the combination of mechanisms that makes this happen is a complex matter.

"Fascination" is another word for idealization, a mental mechanism in which a person attributes exaggeratedly positive qualities to another. Even if they are initially fascinated with a person, a psychopath will inevitably be disappointed as they find out this fascinating object is human and has what they consider flaws and weaknesses, which is intolerable to them. At that point idealization turns into its opposite, devaluation. Devaluation means attributing exaggeratedly negative qualities to another. It is driven by unconscious greed and envy, according to psychopathy expert Dr. Reid Meloy. When the psychopath is envious, he loses his much-needed feelings of superiority and grandiosity. The psychopath's greed and envy cause hatred, and that hatred creates wishes to destroy the object of his or her envy, which in turn eliminates the envy. When envy is eliminated, superiority and grandiosity are temporarily restored.

It is important to understand that envy is hatred of the good object, and greed is the desire to have all the 'contents' of the good object. When greed and demand start again, the cycle must be repeated with a new person.

Meloy says the psychopath must act out this manipulative cycle repetitively and compulsively in order to experience feelings of exhilaration and contempt ("contemptuous delight"), which perpetuate his or her feeling of grandiosity. The manipulative cycle is a 'purification process' for the psychopath, which projects all the bad onto the victim of his manipulation. It is described as a narcissistic repair of the psychopathic process that restores a primitive and defensive equilibrium. They need to do this because their grandiose self is threatened, but must be kept intact.

This process causes a great deal of damage to the victims, who are left confused and devastated.

The psychopath will continue to ward off others by devaluing them, Meloy says, but also continue to seek out new victims. Once a new victim is found, greed and envy cause rage and sadism, and the victim is devalued and destroyed. When that has been accomplished, the psychopath's need for devaluation will start all over again.

They do establish what appear as normal, positive relationships with some people for the purpose of developing a good reputation that covers up their victimization of vulnerable others or that helps them to meet other goals. Many psychopaths are respected and well-liked members of their community because of this. Only those closest to them know the truth.

Seeing that the psychopath is well-liked also serves to make the victim more trusting, and when or if the victim finds out the truth and comes forward, the psychopath is strongly supported by all those who think he or she is a good person. Meanwhile, the victim gets no support or validation—they may have been an unknown who was new to the community or group, or in some other way a marginalized member, which is why the psychopath targeted them in the first place.

It is said that psychopaths know right from wrong, but they just don't care. That's not true.

They are not able to care, so why would it interest them? They don't have the neurological wiring that allows them to care. Their physical brain is different, and those differences leave them without a conscience and without normal emotions or the needs that go with them. They are not able to experience love, so they have no need for love. They know enough about it to inspire it in others in order to take advantage of them, though.

Psychopaths are cunning and intelligent "intra-species predators," according to Dr. Robert Hare, leading psychopathy researcher, creator of the most widely used diagnostic assessment, and author of the book *Without Conscience*.

Hare writes, "They appear to function reasonably well—as lawyers, doctors, psychiatrists, academics, police officers, cult leaders, military personnel, businesspeople, writers, artists, entertainers and so forth—without breaking the law, or at least without being caught and convicted. These individuals are every bit as egocentric, callous and manipulative as the average criminal psychopath; however, their intelligence, family background, social skills and circumstances permit them to construct a façade of normalcy and to get what they want with relative impunity. These subcriminal psychopaths rarely go to prison or any other facility."

If you're targeted and lured into love with a psychopath, you'll be left in ruins while he or she goes on to the next victim with no care or concern for you. There is no easy way to detect them, but awareness may help.

Psychopaths are cunning and calculating predators.

Some go for a vulnerable person who is lonely or has experienced multiple life stressors, such as an illness, a death in the family, or unemployment; this is the easy target. Just desiring a relationship is enough to create the required vulnerability. No one is immune. Psychopaths are adept shape-shifters and changelings able to read their prey like a book. They figure out exactly what you need and they cut the master key that disarms all of your defenses.

It is estimated there are 1-2 psychopaths per 100 people in the population. And they get around. One psychopath can wreak havoc on many through serial "romantic" relationships. It doesn't take long for the psychopath to inflict harm, and he or she can move swiftly and simultaneously among many victims. He can also keep one victim for a long period while having many more on the side. Some maintain a marriage to give the illusion of normalcy. Many psychopaths feast greedily on a banquet of easy targets while taking the time necessary to break down the defenses of more challenging ones.

Psychopaths are notoriously hypersexual and promiscuous; at any one time they may be having sex with their main victim while juggling a few other regulars, having one-night stands with people of either sex, or hiring prostitutes. Psychopaths are most likely to be those who continue to have unprotected sex despite knowing they are HIV positive, according to research.

When you've met someone who you believe is your soul mate and the love of your life, it's not usually the time you think of danger or want consider taking things slowly. After all, this is someone you love and trust. But this is exactly when you need to keep your eyes open and think critically about who this person really is and what they really want. Unfortunately, feeling someone is your soul mate is a red flag warning, because psychopaths are able to so perfectly mirror you and figure out your needs and desires that they appear to be the perfect person for you.

This conundrum is precisely why so many jump headfirst and wholeheartedly into relationships with psychopaths. Unfortunately, what starts out as heaven will turn into hell.

2

THE MASK OF THE PSYCHOPATH... AND WHAT LIES BENEATH

The psychopath has only the vaguest sense of identity (if there is any at all), and therefore he or she has no fixed personality. Instead, they assume whatever persona will work to get them whatever it is they want.

An identity restricts a person to acting in ways that are in accordance with the characteristics of that identity. For example, if someone is (or at least believes that he is) shy or reserved, he will have a hard time being outgoing in most situations.

Since the psychopath lacks a firm identity, he is totally free from the hindrances an identity confers. Instead of being constrained by believing he a certain way and there's nothing he can do about it— such as introverted, awkward, honest-to-a-fault, self-conscious, too trusting, overly conscientious, prone to depression, unlovable, anxious— he is free to be fluid and flexible, and he knows it. They have no such beliefs and no such constraints, so they can be however, whatever, and whomever they need to be at any given moment in order to get what they want.

Marriage counselor Gary Cundiff, MFT, describes how psychopaths use their ability to create a mask to create what victims believe is a "soul mate" relationship. He says that psychopaths select targets based on their best qualities. Then, the predators morph themselves into copies of their targets, so that they appear to be perfect partners.

Cundiff goes on to say that they use each piece of information they gather about us to create a disguise—a mask—that's carefully constructed to look like just like us, their target. They mirror back to us the best aspects of our personalities, while eliminating the flaws and shortcomings.

"The pathological relationship is a one-dimensional interaction. You fall in love with yourself as presented by this reflecting object." This makes the attraction irresistible, since we are attracted to people who are similar to us. This makes the psychopath highly alluring and causes us give him a high degree of trust."

As a result, Cundiff says, "You experience a sense of oneness like none other." The connection that results is intense and addictive.

When the psychopath wants something, he goes for it. When you want something you often *don't* go for it, because you're restrained by some "way that you are" that you believe you can't overcome. But if there was no "way that you are," you would have the freedom to go for what you want with ease. This is what enables the psychopath to fearlessly pursue what he wants.

Being free of internal constraints gives the psychopath the ability to wear a persona like a mask. The psychopath is an actor and most of the time he is skilled, but sometimes things are off just a bit. The facial expression may not be quite right. Maybe he's expressing sorrow, but the corners of his mouth are turned up just a little bit too much. Or maybe he says something that seems rehearsed. But most of the time, they come close enough to fool most people most of the time.

It's widely accepted that the psychopath wears a mask. But just what exactly is underneath it?

It's much simpler than you could imagine, yet it will make your blood run cold. It's very simple, as a matter of fact. Shockingly, stunningly simple.

But first things first.

Why does the psychopath wear a mask in the first place? Because he has little to no identity? True, that gives him the freedom to be whomever or whatever he wants to be. But why is he the way he is, and what does he do with it?

The psychopath is born without the ability to love, without the ability to feel compassion, and without the ability to feel remorse. He is born without a conscience. This is the foundation of miswired neural groundwork that makes possible the predator that is the psychopath.

This basic structure perpetuates a domino effect of other characteristics. First, the psychopath sees as weaknesses the abilities to experience love and remorse. After all, they cause vulnerability and they hold you back from what you might truly desire because you are concerned with other people's well-being. But the psychopath, who is ruthless (which means going after what you want with single-minded focus and with no concern for anything or anyone that gets in the way) sees you as a chump who can be easily manipulated.

Because he sees you as weak and he values ruthlessness, he sees himself as superior to you. All psychopaths are narcissists (although not all narcissists are psychopaths; garden-variety narcissists are believed to have an underlying inferiority complex, while the psychopath has no such thing and is not even capable of it).

But it doesn't just end with feeling superior; the psychopath feels his superiority gives him the right to prey on those whom he believes are inferior.

And the domino effect goes further still! Since the psychopath is incapable of bonding with others because he can't feel love or compassion, and since he feels no remorse for his bad behavior (even though he is completely aware that what he is doing is wrong), his motivations and goals are completely and wholly different from ours. So different, in fact, that it is hard for us to grasp the psychopath's reality, which is another world we can never truly know. The psychopath's motivation is simply self-gratification.

Life is a game for the psychopath, and it's one he or she plays to win. And "win" they will, almost every time, although it's only a win looking through their skewed lens.

Many say the psychopath has no ability to empathize, but he most certainly does. If he didn't know what it was like to be in your shoes, he couldn't know what you were thinking or feeling, which is information he needs to know how to manipulate you. But the empathy he feels is known as "cold empathy" or cognitive empathy – he *understands* what you feel, but he can't *feel* the feeling himself or experience any compassion for it, as someone capable of "warm empathy" would. His cold empathy only serves to provide him with information he can use to victimize you.

So the psychopath wears a mask to hide his true self while he preys on others. But what exactly is under the mask? What is there when there is no persona, no act, and no performance? What lies beneath? Who or what is the "real" psychopath?

To see the psychopath unmasked is to see what he truly is, at his core. It is unmistakable. What it is cannot be accepted or understood and yet at the same time it is immediately identifiable, not at the level of language or the mind, but at the level of the gut. It is a simple primordial knowing that is instantaneous and without doubt.

At his core, all that a psychopath is—the only thing that he is—is a predator. Everything else is the mask. *Everything.*

When the mask drops, the person you thought he or she was disappears. He will look quite different, and any illusion of normalcy will be gone.

You will immediately know, in your bones, that this is predator, and nothing more than that. You will experience what it is to be prey.

The moment you realize he is a predator, you'll know that everything else was merely window dressing, smoke and mirrors, fluff. That was the sheep's clothing, and this is the wolf beneath.

If you're lucky he puts the mask back on, along with the charm that comes with it. But even so, you will never be the same.

3

PSYCHOPATH AS GIGOLO

The central theme of Don Juan's seductions is not even the sexual enjoyment, but playing the trick.

Gordon Banks, "Don Juan as Psychopath"

Right after I was caught in the psychopath's web, he made an unsolicited promise:

"I promise you, I'm no gigolo."

Just like most unsolicited promises[1], it was broken.

The psychopath goes for serial sexual partnerships that are exploitative and shallow. Since the psychopath has no ability to love, he or she isn't looking for a real relationship. And since he has no conscience and can't feel remorse, he thinks nothing of doing whatever it takes to get what he wants. Add to this his charm and complete lack of social anxiety, and what you get is the seducer other men or women can only dream of being.

When a psychopath spots his sexual target, he has no inhibitions that stop him from approaching her. He isn't worried about what to say or what she'll think of him, so he goes for it; what has he got to lose? Fears that hold normal people back don't even enter a psychopath's mind.

Psychoanalyst Ethel Spector Person writes, "The psychopath's insight is always directed toward his internal needs. These needs are not what they appear to be. He is not predominantly hedonistic, although some of his behavior, particularly sexual, might lead one to think so. Instead, he is motivated primarily by the need to dominate and humiliate either the person he is 'taking' or, very often, someone connected to a person with whom he is involved. He may, for instance, seduce a friend's girlfriend."

Dr. Robert Hare describes psychopaths as "intraspecies predators who use charm, manipulation, intimidation, sex and violence to control others and to satisfy their own selfish needs. Lacking in conscience and empathy, they take what they want and do as they please, violating social norms and expectations without guilt or remorse."

Although all of this sounds extremely unattractive, the psychopath can appear as incredibly attractive for the very qualities that make him psychopathic. This is not as contradictory as it sounds. A person whom we sense is not constrained by the same inhibitions, doubts and sensitivities that plague the rest of us can come across as attractive. They have an aura of relaxed confidence and freedom, things many of us want but do not have. They are usually great fun to be with because they take risks and seek new experiences and sensations in order to avoid their nemesis, boredom.

Hare says that the psychopath's lack of ability to attach to others and his shallowness of emotions are behind his compulsion to have sex for sex's sake.

Psychopaths are hypersexual and have high numbers of sexual partners. Because they are less inhibited than the rest of us, they seek thrilling and often dangerous sexual situations. The risky sexual behaviors they engage in put them (and you) at risk for sexually transmitted diseases.

When the psychopath's charm doesn't work, he may become sexually coercive. If he is turned down he may get you intoxicated or use physical force to get his way, according to a study at the University of Central Lancashire.

1 An important note: An unsolicited promise is a promise made when no promise is asked for. It usually means that promise will be broken. For example, an unsolicited "I promise I'll leave you alone after this" commonly means you won't be left alone. "I promise I won't hurt you" usually means that person intends to hurt you, according to *"The Gift of Fear"*, an excellent book by Gavin De Becker.

PSYCHOPATHS AND LOVE

4

PSYCHOPATH AS CHARMER

"Good Morning Red Riding Hood", said Mr. Wolf.

One mustn't look into the abyss, because there is at the bottom an inexplicable charm which attracts us.

Gustave Flaubert

Charm. What is it, and why is the charm of the psychopath so powerful?

I'm not sure where the following description of charm came from originally, but I think it fits quite well:

"Originally a charm was a spell, literally words of an incantation. Then it came to mean an amulet or something worn on the person to ward off evil. From there it became a pretty trinket. It is also an attribute that exerts a fascinating or attractive influence, exciting love or admiration. It is a fascinating quality; charmingness. Charming means fascinating; highly pleasing or delightful to the mind or senses."

The psychopath's charm is like a spell, one that's very hard to break. It's a charm that relaxes defenses, allays fear, paralyzes the mind and induces trance.

What is the source of this charm, and how does it work?

This super-charm is one of the most important tools of the psychopath, one they are able to use very well. The reason they're so good at being charming is their utterly rapt focus on you. It's the focus of a predator on his prey, adorned with a smile. Literally.

The reason the psychopath can focus so powerfully on you is that he's not in his head — he's in yours.

Allow me to explain, if I can.

First, the psychopath has zero distractions, which is extremely unusual. Again, he has the intense focus of a predator on his prey. And unlike a normal person meeting someone new, he's not bothered by things like social anxiety, self-doubt and insecurity. Those things don't exist for him, so they don't get in the way. In other words, the psychopath is not lost in his head like most of us are, thinking thoughts that prevent us from being totally present and prevent us from really connecting with another person. Of course we do connect with others, but it usually takes some time to feel we've connected deeply. But the psychopath is able to create that connection — actually, the illusion of that connection — quickly, sometimes in just a couple of minutes.

After an encounter with his potent charm, you feel you've met someone you're destined to have a profound relationship with (and you will, but not in the way you imagined). Why is that? It's because the ONLY thing on the psychopath's mind is YOU. When the psychopath's high-beam of charm is on you, he is absolutely present. When that presence is focused on you, it's fascinating. Charming, actually. And we're simply not used to that level of "presence." We're not used to being the subject of such intensely focused attention, and that is very compelling in and of itself. Combined with the psychopath's ability to act in a tailor-made way that's perfect for the victim, the experience becomes mesmerizing.

It's the focus of a predator on his prey, adorned with a smile. Literally.

And because that presence is combined with an intense desire that needs to be gratified, the charm is on another level entirely. As one victim of a psychopath said, "The sun shines on you, and it's glorious." Light is a common theme in descriptions of the psychopath's charm. It's like an entrancing beam of light you can't turn away from, and sometimes the wattage is turned up so high that it's blinding.

Second, when you're talking, the psychopath is never busy thinking of what he'll say next. His response depends entirely on listening very closely to you so he can reply in whatever way that gets him what he wants. That's the psychopath's only goal in having a conversation with you. The only reason he wants to get to know you is to find out how to manipulate you. He turns on the charm—which is his generic (but very effective) all-purpose mask—while he creates the perfect mask just for you, the persona that will enable him to get what he wants from you.

What I'm really describing here is an extreme form of lying. Everything the psychopath says is a lie told for the simple purpose of steering you in the direction he wants you to go. If he tells you the truth from time to time, it's only because it will work to steer you in the direction he wants you to go. There's nothing more to it than that. It is pure, unadulterated, manipulation created almost automatically in the psychopath's mind.

Many of us learned the hard way that when you knock on a psychopath's door, no one is home. There's a reason for that.

This also explains the psychopath's "sixth sense" ability to read people so well, that uncanny ability he has to easily see who is vulnerable, to know which target will respond to him, to know just the right words to say, to quickly learn your deepest desires so he can pretend to fulfill them, and to learn your deepest fears and insecurities so he can assume the most control. The psychopath's sixth sense — and his charm — come directly from his abilities to be completely present, to focus completely on his prey and to have self-gratification as his only goal.

How charming is that?

5

RED FLAGS OF A PSYCHOPATH

"Why is the seduction of the psychopath so powerful? Because it is the art of the con wrapped in the beautiful illusion of love."

Author unknown

Psychopaths aren't capable of love, but that doesn't stop them from involving unsuspecting people in pseudo-relationships that have devastating consequences.

If you can spot a psychopath early in a relationship, you can to avoid the serious harm they will inevitably bring to you and your life. None of the signs on the list below can stand on its own, but together they paint an overall picture that serves as a warning you should heed. When you're involved in it, though, it may seem like the best thing that has ever happened to you, which makes it hard to discern between having fallen in love or fallen for a psychopath.

Red Flags

He or she is incredibly charming, in exactly the way YOU find charming. Need someone confident, outgoing and warm? The psychopath can do that. Need someone sensitive and a bit bumbling, but with a heart of gold? He can do that, too. This charm causes you—his target—to fall under his spell while he focuses intensely on you. His focus is very pleasing to the mind and senses, and it disables your personal boundaries, your gut instincts and your self-protective behavior. It induces a trance-like sate; a pleasant, relaxed and focused state of mind that leaves you open to suggestion. You will find yourself wanting to be back in the focus of his or her potent charm again and again.

This superhuman charm is the first early red flags of a psychopath, and it is exactly what makes it hard to walk away. This charm stems from the psychopath's ability to be completely present as they focus on you while they figure out what makes you tick, what flattery you long to hear and what buttons to push. You'll feel like the two of you are the only things in the universe, and that you've finally find someone who appreciates you, understands you and sees the good qualities in you that others too often overlook.

He is very much at ease; he may have a demeanor of being anxiety-free and without any social awkwardness. Very comfortable in his own skin. His ease puts you at ease and you feel comfortable with him, like the two of you have known each other forever. He's not necessarily attention-grabbing or the life of the party, but he is very socially skilled. Some psychopaths may come across as down-to-earth and humble while still maintaining a distinct aura of confidence and presence.

He or she is a glib, smooth talker who never runs out questions to ask you or amusing anecdotes, and can make the most mundane topics seem interesting and entertaining. The purpose of this is to relax you and make you comfortable with him.

He or she will quickly divulge personal details and stories about their life. This will create a false sense of intimacy that causes you to reciprocate with details about your own life so it will seem like you two are getting close. After all, you've both shared personal things; you've both risked judgment and rejection by being vulnerable, yet you've supported and accepted each other.

He or she is fun-loving and fun to be with. Psychopaths are playful. They hate to be bored, so you won't be bored when you're with one. You'll never before have had so much fun with anyone. You'll do things you never did before, maybe even just little adventures that take you away from the mundane, and you'll realize how small and boring your life had become, and how stale the world had seemed. You've come back to life, and you didn't even know you needed to. Or maybe you did know it, and now along comes the perfect person to help you do it!

He or she claims to be a happy, easy going person, and sure seems like one. He may tell you nothing gets him down. Since a psychopath has no conscience and no anxiety it's probably true, but you'll see it in a different way and just be happy you haven't ended up with yet another neurotic mate weighed down by a load of emotional baggage.

He or she is a very active person who is always on the go. He needs a lot of stimulation and can't tolerate boredom, so he can't stand being alone or sitting still.

You'll feel very special in his or her presence and feel that he's very special, fascinating and unique, and not like anyone you've known before.

You'll find yourself becoming deeply enamored with him or her very quickly, in a way you haven't previously experienced. You'll attribute this to the special nature of the relationship you believe is forming.

The psychopath looks at you in a way no one has before; he keeps his eyes on you and gives you his complete attention. It feels flattering and seductive. You'll have never before felt so beautiful, handsome or sexy. You'll feel very good about yourself in his or her presence. Your insecurities about attractiveness and likeability will vanish as if they never existed as the psychopath appears to recognize and appreciate all of your good qualities.

You will become intensely physically attracted to him or her, more than you have ever felt with anyone else or even knew was possible.

The psychopath will shower you with attention and affection. You'll go on frequent romantic dates and spend a lot of time together. You'll get plenty of phone calls, emails and text messages. He or she will be kind, considerate and complimentary. You may feel truly appreciated by someone for the first time in your life. It's all positive reinforcement all the time during this early stage, which is called "love bombing." You will not feel neglected in any way at this point. He or she always makes time for you. Although things may seem unusually intense, it will just convince you that this is the best relationship you've ever had and that he or she is your perfect partner. The manipulator will saturate you in as many ways possible with love and adoration; you won't have a moment to come up for air. There will be many verbal declarations of their feelings for you and all your wonderful qualities, and amazement at all the things you have in common and at how lucky you both are to have found each other. You'll believe it's the best thing that ever happened to you, so you won't even suspect you're being played.

The psychopath will divulge their "true" feelings for you very quickly, telling you they love you and have never experienced such love and attraction before or that they never thought they'd fall in love again. He or she will claim once-in-a-lifetime love, the type that's written on the stars and dictated by destiny. Your days of unrequited love will seem like they're finally over. The relationship will feel... magical. You'll feel like you are finally experiencing what it means to have found your soul mate, even if you didn't believe that soul mates existed. You'll feel that you never knew what love was before. You may have only known him or her for a very short amount of time -- maybe a few weeks -- but you'll be certain that the two of you will be together forever. Believing someone is your soul mate is, unfortunately, one of the biggest red flags of a psychopath.

> "In the desert, an old monk once advised a traveler that the voices of God and the Devil are barely distinguishable."
>
> Loren Eiseley

If you've gotten this far, there's a good chance the psychopath has already created the strong bond (the psychopathic bond) that is the necessary foundation for the manipulation and abuse that will follow. The only thing that can stop it is awareness of the possibility that your soul mate might not be who you think he or she is, and this awareness may help you retain your abilities to think critically. Easier said than done! It will seem like the love story you've been longing for all your life, and even better than anything you could have imagined.

So, how can you tell the difference between real love and a psychopathic charade? It is difficult, but there is hope. Here are some recommendations that may help you avoid involvement with a psychopath:

- Take any new relationship slowly, especially an intense one. Control the pace, as opposed to letting the other person control it. Know what you want from a relationship so you don't become obliviously sucked into following someone else's agenda. Be leery of someone who gets serious quickly. How can someone love you deeply and know they want to be with you forever if they barely know you? That's often the mark of superficiality, which is in direct contrast from what it may look like. There is no rush. Time is the only thing that will reveal a person's true character. Time is your friend.

- Know your personal boundaries -- or develop them if you don't have any -- and be aware of a person who is able to make you disregard those boundaries, even if you believe you're the one deciding to do so. Boundaries do not isolate you from others -- they only protect you from manipulative people who do not respect you or have your best interests at heart (to say the least). They let the good in while keeping the bad out. Become clear about yours and make the decision to guard them. Psychopaths will push your boundaries as a "test" to see what they can get away with and to lower your defenses, while a good person who is truly interested in you will respect them. Boundaries are not manipulations or tests—they are your (sincere) limits as to what you are comfortable with and what you will tolerate.

- Know yourself well. If you don't, a psychopath will know you better than you do, which sets you up for trouble. Find out what runs you, process traumas from your past and identify your deepest fears, desires and needs. This is one of the best defenses.

- Expect someone to earn your trust…and then expect them to keep earning it. Being trustworthy is an ongoing thing. Keep in mind that con artists are masters at gaining your trust; that's why they're so effective. Psychopaths are the ultimate cons.

- Know what you want and need from a relationship, and don't settle for anything less. If you do find yourself settling for less when things take a turn for the worse, you'll know something is wrong.

- Delay sex because once you have it, your neurochemistry will shift and you will feel deeper attraction, a craving for your partner and more investment in the relationship. Pacing and slowing down lets you keep control and make clear-headed decisions. It is much easier to see reality and much easier to walk away from someone you haven't yet had sex with. Sex seals the deal. Is delaying sex realistic when you're faced with someone you think is your soul mate and you're feeling intense attraction? That will be up to you to decide.

The red flags sound like the description of two people falling deeply in love. That's exactly why so many have fallen victim. Obviously, no one is going to fall in love and just see it as one big red flag and walk away, and I'm not saying that's what you should do. But those of us who have experienced it know that it was over-the-top, "unreal," magical and unlike anything we had ever experienced. Those are the signs that tell you that you need to keep your eyes open.

Staying alert can help prevent an entanglement with a psychopath while still preserving the opportunity to move forward with a person who has honest intentions.

"Many spiritual traditions recognize that when the dark one appears he is most beautiful, most wonderful and most engaging. The truth only comes out later."

Author unknown

6

STAGES OF THE PSYCHOPATHIC BOND

The predictable yet completely unexpected and devastating pattern of a relationship with a psychopath is broken down into three stages: Idealize, Devalue and Discard.

This relationship starts out like heaven on earth…but ends in a place worse than hell.

When you're targeted by a psychopath and deemed a suitable victim for his or her or her game of power, control, and self-gratification, stage one—the idealization stage—begins. You think you're entering an exciting, romantic relationship and that you've met the love of your life... but what you're actually entering is a game that you're guaranteed to lose. The object of the game: He or she will gain control, harm you, take what he wants, and leave you an emotional wreck.

The psychopath lures you with charm, attention, flattery, and other covert emotional manipulation tactics. He will say anything to get what he wants because he's a pathological liar, and what he wants at this point is to win your love and trust. His or her loving persona is a complete fabrication. Even so, you'll believe that you're "soul mates" because he's able to present himself as your perfect partner.

This stage is often called "Love Bombing." The manipulator will saturate his or her target in as many ways possible with love and adoration, without a moment to come up for air. They'll spend as much time as possible with the target and keep in frequent contact. There will be many verbal declarations of appreciation and of their feelings for you and all your wonderful qualities, and they will express amazement at all the things you have in common or at how lucky you both are to have found each other. You'll believe it's the best thing that ever happened to you, so you won't even suspect you're being played. The manipulator may tell you he or she believes you're "soul mates" or say "isn't this magical?" or tell you that you must have known each other in a past life.

"What the psychopath does is they weave a picture of a person that's really a dream. It's a spirit. It's not real. You feel like you've discovered a soul mate. Once you're in that bond—and we call it the psychopathic bond—you don't want to break it," according to Paul Babiak, PhD, psychopathy expert and author of the book, Snakes in Suits: When Psychopaths Go to Work.

The psychopath is not able to bond with another human, but he is good at getting others to bond to him. This is known as the psychopathic bond. The whole idealization stage is a sham the psychopath creates intentionally in order to create that bond, which makes you vulnerable to the manipulation and abuse that will follow.

He or she never idealized you as a person; you were only idealized as an object of desire, one to use, denigrate, and discard. He was never interested in you; he was only interested in gaining control over you, manipulating you, harming you and getting what he could from you. As such, his interest was shallow and short-lived, and he moves on to new sources of diversion and pleasure. It's too bad that by the time this happens, you've already pinned your expectations, hopes and dreams onto him or her.

The perfect "honeymoon" stage lasts until the psychopath becomes bored with you (and he'll get bored quickly once he knows you're hooked). At this point, he has no incentive to hide his true nature any longer, so stage two — the devaluation stage — begins. You believed you were once the center of his life, but you sense he's pulling away. The psychopath is skilled at what's known as "dosing," which is giving you just enough attention and validation to keep you on his hook. He begins to change the game to one of giving you just enough positive reinforcement to keep from losing you, while pushing your boundaries further, gradually and steadily devaluing you and taking you lower. You'll find yourself tolerating continually worsening treatment, which diminishes your self-respect.

> "The more infrequently the crumbs of love are offered, the more hooked you are. You become conditioned, like a rat in a cage."

As you become less exciting to him, he devalues you even more. You stay because he or she has manipulated you into thinking less of yourself and accepting poor treatment, and you stay because you're still holding onto the memory of your love from the idealization stage. Fearful of losing that completely, you try hard to fix things and you tolerate increasingly worse behavior. You'll experience cognitive dissonance as the truth about him comes into your conscious mind, but is battled by your denial; your thoughts ping-pong back and forth relentlessly as you try to figure out what's really going on.

During the devaluation stage, he will use an arsenal of covert emotional manipulation tactics to keep you under his control, to keep you doubting yourself, to keep you putting up with his deplorable behavior and to keep you believing his lies. Learn about these tactics so you have a better chance of recognizing them. No one is immune, especially when a strong emotion like love is involved.

Because your self-esteem has been lowered so drastically, you blame yourself for not being enough for him or for having another woman in his life. He doesn't take responsibility for his own behavior, and blames everything—including the demise of the relationship—on you.

And in your state of mind, you believe it.

"From beginning to end, all this phony relationship can offer you is a toxic combination of fake love and real abuse. He constructs the psychopathic bond through deception and manipulation. You maintain it through self-sacrifice and denial," writes Claudia Moscovici on her website, PsychopathyAwareness.

Now comes stage three, when he or she discards you. He's gotten everything he wanted from you—including your self-respect, your happiness, and your dignity. You may have also lost friends, family, and finances as the relationship took over your life.

"The psychopath discards his ex-lovers with a degree of vitriol and hatred that astonishes his victims and exceeds any boundaries of normality," says Moscovici

You may be the one who finally puts an end to it and walks away. Either way, you come to the realization the entire relationship was a fraud from day one. It was a betrayal in the purest sense of the word. Along with betrayal, the victimized person feels deep disappointment, profound loss, anger, bewilderment and incredulity.

The stages of the psychopathic bond are what describes emotional rape, which is devastating. Some people find little understanding or support from those who are close to them, because others often see it as a typical 'love gone wrong' situation. It is far more than that. Please make sure you get the help you need to recover from this experience.

7
EMOTIONAL RAPE

"Ours were false relationships from the very beginning in which we were targeted, exploited and betrayed."

Donna Anderson, LoveFraud

The quote above gets right to the heart of the matter of emotional rape. These were never normal relationships that started with love and then just went wrong. Far from it. The psychopath is a predator who completely hides his or her true identity and motives as they target a victim with the intent of causing harm.

Contrary to what many believe, psychopaths are not primarily out to use a victim for sex or anything else. Their goals are to dominate, control and humiliate so they can diminish and devalue their victim, which feeds their pathological grandiosity. Using the victim is only secondary.

In a profound act of betrayal, he only pretends to love her—and does a convincing job of it—in order to gain her love and trust, which is what makes carrying out his hidden agenda possible. He gains power and control through manipulation tactics and uses her for whatever he desires without any remorse, while he creates an ever-worsening emotional hell. His grandiosity swells as he watches her try in vain to save the relationship she truly believed was the best one of her life.

The predator gets bored with her after devaluing and diminishing her, and he needs the thrill of a fresh new victim. The predator ends the relationship with a stunning and completely abnormal display of contempt as his final expression of callous disregard. If he is using the relationship to provide an illusion of normalcy, he may stick around long-term. If the victim ends the relationship, his grandiosity will suffer and he will attempt to gain her trust again. A psychopath hates to lose control of a victim.

She is devastated as she comes to realize his love was never real and that he purposefully and heartlessly betrayed her. If she doesn't realize it—and many victims don't understand what really happened until years later, if ever—she blames herself, which makes healing difficult or even impossible.

Either way, she is left with a heart, soul and psyche ravaged by the predator.

The aftermath of emotional rape often includes rage, obsessive thoughts, lost self-esteem, fear, anxiety, the inability to love or trust, use of alcohol or drugs, physical illness, and irrational and extreme behavior such as total isolation and withdrawal or even suicide, according to Sandra Brown, M.A., who treats women who have been victimized.

A lack of support from friends and family makes things much worse. Some will blame her for choosing to have a relationship with a "jerk," because they don't know or can't believe he was a predator capable of hiding his true identity. Some blame her for staying with him when she knew it was going bad, because they are unaware or unwilling to believe she was controlled like a puppet by his systematic manipulation. Others who fell for the psychopath's charisma and powers of persuasion may blame her for losing a "good catch." Whatever the case, no one realizes how severely traumatized she really is.

The trauma is severe, and the victim should pursue professional psychological help from a therapist familiar with abusive relationships and the trauma they cause.

Aftermath: Surviving Psychopathy, a website founded by David Kosson, Ph.D., professor of psychology and psychopathy researcher, was created to provide help as well as education to those whose lives have been impacted by psychopathic individuals It warns:

"Sadly, some victims of psychopaths attempt suicide as a result of hopelessness, helplessness and the belief there is no way out. Some have reported to us that psychopaths have actually encouraged them to take their own lives or have indicated that they would put them through so much turmoil that their only recourse would be suicide."

Even if you feel hopeless now, don't give up. Many people have recovered from psychopathic abuse. If you are feeling suicidal, please get help immediately.

8

COVERT EMOTIONAL MANIPULATION

"Until you realize how easily it is for your mind to be manipulated, you remain the puppet of someone else's game."

Evita Ochel

Covert emotional manipulation occurs when a person who wants to gain power and control over you uses deceptive and underhanded tactics to change your thinking, behavior and perceptions. Emotional manipulation operates under the level of your conscious awareness. It holds you psychologically captive. Victims usually don't realize what's going on while it's happening.

A skilled emotional manipulator gets you to put your sense of self-worth and emotional well-being into his hands. Once you make that grave mistake, he methodically and continually chips away at your identity and self-esteem until there's little left.

How can you tell if you're a victim? For help, read the blog post "How to Tell if You're Being Manipulated." It's wise to be aware of the many tactics manipulators can use against you. But if you want to know if you're being manipulated, you need only recognize the effects of manipulation in yourself.

This website is concerned with the most dangerous manipulators — psychopaths — who see themselves as superior and see others as nothing more than prey to be hunted to fulfill their needs. They have no ability to love, no empathy, no guilt or remorse, and no conscience. To the psychopath, life is a "game" of taking power and control and getting what they want, such as sex, money or influence, and attempting to destroy the victim emotionally, psychologically, spiritually or physically in the process. This is nothing more than entertainment to them. When they're bored and filled with contempt for you (e.g. when they've "won the game") they move on to the next victim.

Others use manipulation tactics too, such as narcissists, sociopaths, etc. It's harmful, no matter who is doing it.

These highly skilled covert manipulators are incapable of having a real relationship, and many set out from day one with a plan. They are adept at reading you and quickly learn your weaknesses, your strengths, your fears, your dreams and your desires. They won't hesitate to use all of these against you with an arsenal of effective manipulation tactics carefully chosen and personalized just for you. Manipulators hunger for power and control and they will stop at nothing to get them, even if this means harming you.

If you feel less strong, less confident, less secure, less intelligent, less sane, or in any other way "less than" anything you were before, you are being covertly emotionally manipulated.

Just when you believe the magical excitement of a loving relationship has made a welcome and long-awaited appearance in your life, something very different and sinister might actually be in the works. Psychopaths are highly skilled at hiding their real personalities and their real plans. Their goal is to trick you into believing they love you — and they do everything they can to make you believe that during a non-stop phase of romantic magic. This intense bonding stage is created for one reason — to hook you and make you vulnerable to the manipulation and abuse that will follow.

The purpose of your relationship will change from loving you to demeaning, degrading and exploiting you, confusing you, and diminishing your self-respect, self-worth, and self-esteem. The psychopath will make just enough appearances as the wonderful, loving guy or gal you fell in love with to keep you hooked, to keep you blaming yourself for losing the best thing you ever had and to keep you willing to do anything to save the relationship.

You'll accept mere crumbs if that will prove your love. You'll stop wasting time discussing your needs, emotions and fears, which he doesn't care about and considers unacceptable weaknesses. You'll blame yourself for things going wrong, analyzing every word and every mood, going over every conversation, and becoming very confused about what's really going on. Your life, your job, your relationships with others, and your physical and mental health will suffer.

He keeps you around until you're the desperate mess he manipulated you into becoming. When that happens, he will announce — with feigned or real vitriol, disdain and seething contempt — that you bore him and he's done with you. You'll be left an emotional wreck wondering how things went so terribly wrong…wondering how your soul-mate relationship went from heaven-on-earth straight into the bowels of hell.

Victims of this underhanded and deceptive manipulation struggle with feelings of confusion and severe emotional pain. Many also experience obsessive thoughts, rage, lost self-esteem, insomnia, anxiety, panic, fear, an inability trust, use of alcohol or drugs, lack of support, and physical illness. Irrational and sometimes extreme behavior can occur, such as isolation and withdrawal from friends, family and society, and suicidal thoughts or actions.

The hard truth is that the psychopath never wanted love. You were targeted by a predator for the purpose of victimization, and the plan for your harm was there when he targeted you and found you receptive to his advances. After all is said and done and you're lying alone in the rubble, you realize something was horribly wrong.

When someone starts a relationship pretending to love you but really wants to hurt you, you have been the victim of emotional rape, a heinous moral crime. You will not find help from information and support designed for getting over a normal relationship.
How did the most loving and beautiful relationship of your life turn into the worst relationship of your life? The answer is contained in three words: covert emotional manipulation.

Covert emotional manipulation methodically wears down your sense of self-worth and self-confidence, and destroys your trust in your own perceptions.

How can you tell if you're being covertly manipulated?

Emotional manipulation can be so subtle and undercover that it can control you for a long time before you figure out what's happening, if you ever do at all. Some manipulators are highly skilled. They're described as puppet masters, and you could unknowingly become a puppet if you don't know the signs.

As your strings are pulled this way and that, you do just what the puppet master wants you to do. You think you're acting from your own free will, but you are not.

If you're a victim of manipulation you probably know something is wrong, but you're not quite sure what it is. You might even suspect you're being manipulated but you don't know for sure if you are or how it's being done. One thing you do know is that you want answers—are you being manipulated or not? How can you tell?

Actually, it is easier and more obvious than you might think it is.

It's smart to learn the techniques of covert emotional manipulation, but the truth is you don't have to know anything at all about the techniques to know if you're being manipulated. You only need to look at yourself to know if manipulation is at play.

Manipulation is detrimental and has profound negative effects on us, even if we don't know it's happening. Those negative effects are the evidence left when the crime of manipulation has taken place.

If you are in a relationship and notice any of the following signs, there is a high probability you are being manipulated:

- Your joy at finding love has turned into the fear of losing it. Your feelings have gone from happiness and euphoria to anxiety, sadness and even desperation.

- Your mood depends entirely on the state of the relationship, and you are experiencing extreme highs and lows.

- You're unhappy in the relationship and uncertain about it much of the time, yet you dread losing it because you're blissfully happy every now and then.

- You feel like you're responsible for ruining the best thing that ever happened to you, but you're not sure how.

- Your relationship feels very complex, although you're don't know why. When talking to others about it, you might find yourself saying "It's hard to explain. It's just really complicated."

- You continually obsess about the relationship, analyzing every detail repeatedly in a desperate attempt to "figure it out." You talk about it all the time to anyone who will listen. It doesn't do any good.

- You never feel sure of where you stand with your partner, which leaves you in a perpetual state of uncertainty and anxiety.

• You frequently ask your partner if something is wrong. It really does feel as if something's wrong, but you are not sure what it is.

• You are frequently on the defensive. You feel misunderstood and have the need to explain and defend yourself.

• You seem to have developed a problem with trust, jealousy, insecurity, anger or overreaction, which your partner has pointed out to you on many occasions.

• You feel ongoing anger or resentment for someone.

• You have become a detective. You scour the web for information about your partner, keep a close eye on his or her social media accounts, and feel a need to check their web search history, texts or emails. When they are not at home, you have a desire to verify their whereabouts as you worry about where they really are.

• You feel that you don't truly know how to make your partner happy. You try hard but nothing seems to work, at least not for long. You used to make them very happy and you're not sure what's changed.

• Expressing negative thoughts and emotions feels restricted or even forbidden, so you try to keep those things to yourself. You feel frustrated at being unable to talk about things that are bothering you.

• You don't feel as good about yourself as you did before the relationship. You feel less confident, less secure, less intelligent, less sane, less trusting, less attractive or in some other way "less than" what you were before.

• You always feel you're falling short of your partner's expectations. You feel inadequate.

• You often feel guilty and find yourself apologizing a lot. You continually try to repair damage you believe you've caused. You blame yourself for your partner pulling away from you. You can't understand why you keep sabotaging the relationship.

- You carefully control your words, actions and emotions around your partner to keep him or her from withdrawing their affection again.

- At times, you erupt like an emotional volcano filled with anger, frustration and even hostility. You have never acted this way before and vow that you will stop, but no matter how hard you try it keeps happening.

- You do things you aren't really comfortable with or that go against your values, limits or boundaries, in order to make your partner happy and keep the relationship intact.

You should have your answer.

There is one caveat. If your past relationships have had an ongoing pattern of insecurity, mistrust and fear of abandonment, you may have a psychological issue that would benefit from professional intervention.

You might be wondering how you or anyone else could stay in a relationship that causes fear, anxiety, depression, self-doubt, confusion and frustration. Wouldn't you know something is terribly wrong? Why would you stay?

First, these relationships don't start out this way. In fact, the relationship probably got off to an amazing start. He or she seemed like your perfect partner—maybe even your soul mate—and the honeymoon phase was idyllic. When things took a turn for the worse, you had no idea what was really going on. Naturally, you would try to work things out and regain what once was so promising and wonderful. Having been manipulated into blaming yourself for the problems, you hang on and desperately try to repair the damage you believe you caused and regain your partner's love. Your loyalty seems to pay off and you and your partner are once again close and loving... for a while. It becomes a cycle, one you're not fully aware of.

Second, manipulation begins slowly and insidiously, and gradually escalates."Manipulation is an evolving process over time," according to Harriet B. Braiker, PhD., author of *"Who's Pulling Your Strings."*

Braiker says victims are controlled through a series of promised gains and threatened losses, covertly executed through a variety of manipulation tactics. In other words, the manipulation builds gradually as the abuser creates uncertainty and doubt by going back and forth from giving you what you desire to threatening to take it away.

Joe Navarro, M.A., a 25-year veteran of the FBI and author of the book *Dangerous Personalities*, writes "In the end, it doesn't matter how you got into that relationship, it is the realization that it is one-sided, exploitative, and toxic that counts. The questions that need to be asked are very simple. 'Are they using their charms or behavior to control you or others for their own benefit? Are they manipulating you? Are they doing things that hurt you or put you at risk? Do you feel like this relationship is one sided? Are you hurting in this relationship?' If the answer to these questions is yes, it is time to untangle yourself from the toxic strings that control you so you can get your life back. Take heed - you have no social obligation to be victimized – ever."

Emotional manipulation is emotional abuse. A person who controls your feelings and behavior with manipulation does not value or respect you or care about your well-being. Leave the relationship if at all possible, and seek professional counseling if necessary. Involvement with a skilled manipulator can result in serious and lasting harm.

9

THE GAME YOU DIDN'T KNOW YOU WERE PLAYING

When targeted by a psychopath, we unwittingly become an opponent in a game we don't even know we're playing. The stakes are high and the odds are stacked in their favor. They make the rules, and play to win. How could they lose, with such unfair advantages?

On our first official "date," the psychopath who victimized me did something incredible—he told me about the game. He came right out and laid it all out for me. He told me the object of the game, and the outcome. Yes, you read that right—he told me about the game. Of course he didn't say it was a game, but that was the only thing he left out. Like some covert fortune teller, he told me my future. He could predict it because he himself would make it happen.

We sat at a cozy corner table in a romantic restaurant, and his eyes seemed to sparkle as he gazed into mine. Looking sincere and hopeful, he told me he wanted our relationship to get off to a good start and to stay that way. In order to do that, he said, it was imperative that the balance of power remained equal.

I asked him to explain what he was talking about. He told me that relationships go wrong when the balance of power becomes lopsided. When one person cares more than the other, he said, they have less power, while the one who cares less has more power. The one with the most power would control the relationship, while the one with less would be miserable. He went on to say that this imbalance of power would lead to the end of the relationship as the needy, powerless person who cared more drove away the person who cared less. (Notice the two main theme—power and control—exactly the things a psychopath wants.)

I thought about it and it seemed he did have a point, but I asked him why he was worried about it in our case. I told him I was sure that as long as both of us cared about each other, everything would be just fine. We had a very special thing, so there was no reason to think about what might go wrong. He said he was concerned because that very scenario had happened in several of his past relationships (red flag!) and he didn't want it to happen again, especially with me. He said he feared that he cared more, and I assured him it wasn't true.

The conversation only made him more endearing to me as I surmised that he was a thoughtful, sensitive man who was afraid of losing me, who didn't want anything ruining the rare magic we had discovered with each other.

Boy, was I wrong.

I forgot all about that conversation, even as the game played out. I didn't remember it until after it was over, when I stumbled upon this quote somewhere online:

> "This is how they think. It's all about who is in control, who is on top, who has the most power, WHO CARES LESS, WHO CARES LESS, WHO CARES LESS, WHO CARES LESS, WHO CARES LESS. Do I have to repeat it?"

Those words hit me like a ton of bricks. I was made to play a sick game only he knew we were playing. He planned all his moves well in advance, and I played right into his hands.

The Psychopath's Game:

Players: The psychopath and his unsuspecting opponent

Object of the Game: Power and control over the opponent

Strategy: Idealize, devalue, discard

Purpose: Restoration of the psychopath's illusion of grandiosity

The Winner: There is none

Psychopaths are driven to play this "game," over and over, throughout their lives. It's all about devaluation.

Devaluation is driven by unconscious greed and envy, according to psychopathy expert Dr. Reid Meloy. When the psychopath is envious, he loses his much-needed feelings of superiority and grandiosity. The psychopath's greed and envy causes hatred, and that hatred creates wishes to destroy the object of his or her envy, which in turn eliminates the envy. When envy is eliminated, superiority and grandiosity are temporarily restored.

It is important to understand that envy is hatred of the good object, and greed is the desire to have all the 'contents' of the good object.

"What he gets he spoils and wastes; he feels frustrated and deprived, and the greed and demand start again."

When greed and demand start again, the game must be played again.

Meloy says the psychopath must act out this manipulative cycle repetitively and compulsively in order to experience feelings of exhilaration and contempt (contemptuous delight), which perpetuate his feeling of grandiosity. The manipulative cycle is a 'purification process' for the psychopath, which projects all the bad onto the victim of his manipulation. It is described as a narcissistic repair of the psychopathic process that restores a primitive and defensive equilibrium. They need to do this because their grandiose self is threatened, but must be kept intact.

The psychopath will continue to ward off others by devaluing them, Meloy says, but also continue to seek out new victims. Once he finds a victim his greed and envy cause rage and sadism, and the victim is devalued and destroyed. When that has been accomplished, the psychopath's need for devaluation will start all over again, and the game will be played with someone new and equally unsuspecting.

10

INTENSITY OR INTIMACY?

"I was addicted to a high that only my abuser could give me. Because the lower an abuser puts someone, the higher they can elevate them."

Amanda Domuracki, Culture Shock, The Highs and Lows of Emotional Abuse

It seemed that magic had entered our lives. It brought with it once-in-a-lifetime soul-mate love, true romance, amazing sex… We were swept off our feet and taken to an enchanted world just for two, one that floated like a bubble high above the mundane world below.

We never expected that bubble would burst. We believed the incredible intensity we shared indicated a deep connection, one that would last for a lifetime.

Normally, romantic love is an experience that can foster bonding and intimacy. That never happened because we were with someone who was incapable of bonding and intimacy. We didn't even realize those things were missing, because we were dazed and deluded by the extraordinary intensity of our experience and the multitude of lies we were told. Smoke and mirrors distracted us from the truth.

> "I have flown and fallen, and I have swum deep and drowned, but there should be more to love than 'I survived it.'"
>
> Lisa Mantchev, So Silver Bright

Intimacy has to do with trust, understanding, and feeling understood. People who are emotionally intimate reveal vulnerabilities without fear that what they share will be turned against them. Intimacy is based on safety, patience, respect, consistency, and a mutual give-and-take. Without self-disclosure, there can be no intimacy. The more intimate you are with someone, the safer you feel and the more worthwhile the relationship.

> "There is nothing more intimate in life than simply being understood."
>
> Brad Meltzer, The Inner Circle

Intensity, on the other hand, is all about drama, anxiety, uncertainty, and fear. It's all about push-pull, cold-hot, high-low.

According to Harriet Lerner, PhD, in her book *Dance of Intimacy*, "Intensity is being completely lost in the emotion of unreasoning desire. It is marked by urgency, sexual desire, anxiety, high risk choices, and the reckless abandonment of what was once valued. All-consuming euphoria similar to recreational drug use (addictive chemical reactions in the brain) .... loss of ability to make rational evaluations of what is true, valuable and worthy. Desire to be always close to that person at any cost.

An intimate relationship is one in which neither party silences, sacrifices, or betrays the self and each party expresses strength and vulnerability, weakness and competence in a balanced way.

Intimacy means that we can be who we are in a relationship, and allow the other person to do the same. 'Being who we are' requires that we can talk openly about things that are important to us, that we take a clear position on where we stand on important emotional issues, and that we clarify the limits of what is acceptable and tolerable to us in a relationship."

That's simply not possible with a psychopath. They aren't neurologically capable of intimacy and a healthy relationship.

"The most important test of intimacy is to ask yourself the question, 'Is this relationship a safe haven where I feel loved and accepted for being me?'" writes Randi Kreger, author of the srticle, "Problems With Emotional Intimacy—Typical for BPs and NP"

Bonding created by intense emotional highs and lows is maintained by powerful surges of euphoria-inducing dopamine during the highs. During the lows, there is intense craving for more.

Learning theorists have found that a pattern of intermittent reinforcement, which is positive reinforcement alternated with punishment (a pattern of abuse and reward), develops the strongest emotional bonds.

Powerful emotional attachments are seen to develop from two specific features of abusive relationships: power imbalances and intermittent good-bad treatment, according to psychology researchers

Donald G. Dutton and S. Painter, "Emotional attachments in abusive relationships: A test of traumatic bonding theory," Violence and Victims, Volume 8, 1993.

Intermittent good-bad treatment triggers biological changes as well as emotional ones. Going 'cold turkey' (having no contact with him or her) may seem impossible. It is actually the same as an addiction to drugs, alcohol or gambling — all addictions are caused by dopamine. This is why you can't or couldn't stop thinking about them, despite knowing how bad they were for you. This bond is basically a compulsive relationship fostering specific patterns of compulsive behavior — an addiction — not an intimate relationship.

This addictive attachment is known as a Betrayal Bond (or Trauma Bond).

Betrayal bonds are highly addictive attachments to those who have hurt you. Exploitative relationships often become betrayal bonds. A person in a betrayal bond is essentially addicted to the relationship with someone who is destructive and hurtful. Signs of a betrayal bond include the inability to detach and self-destructive denial.

"We cannot walk away, though, because without us realizing it, our abuser has become our human needle; our Drug Lord of Love. The person who owns our self-value and self-worth and who, in the name of love, can reject us into deep lows with a single glare, or send us to euphoric highs with one simple smile," writes Domurack.i

As the relationship goes on, the less safe you feel. That's a red flag that there is something really wrong.

Domuracki says, "Your life is loaned to you through an abuser. It is on his or her whim that you thrive, struggle, hope, and fear. In abuse, you can endure a thousand losses for a single, shimmering penny that proves you've won something."

Brene Brown, sociologist and expert on social connection, conducted thousands of interviews to find the root of deep social connection. An analysis of the data revealed that it was vulnerability. Vulnerability here does not mean being weak. On the contrary—what it means is the courage to be yourself. It involves uncertainty, exposure, and risk. We may want to run from vulnerability, but it is an inevitable part of social relationships that are to become close and rewarding.

Emotional intimacy comes from being vulnerable enough to allow yourself to be fully known, and to be accepted and understood when you do. That creates the potential for true intimacy. It does come with the risk of rejection, but if you're rejected you'll know that you're not a relationship you should continue.

To know that you are loved for who you are, and to know someone else in all of their vulnerability and to love them as they are, may be one of life's most fulfilling experiences. Intensity, on the other hand, is the opposite of fulfilling. It's draining, exhausting, crazymaking, and ultimately empty.

In future relationships we can ask ourselves, "Is this real intimacy or just intensity?"

11

KNOW WHAT YOU WANT AND NEED

When we imagining our ideal relationship, none of us thinks:

"I want to be in an unhappy relationship with a person who is only out to dominate and humiliate me, and who is only interested in self-gratification. Ideally, he'll be someone who has no respect for me and who will manipulate me into losing all respect for myself. He must be able to take control of me so he can hurt me deeply and repeatedly, and yet keep me running back for more with just a few kind words or a worn-out promise. I want him to be a pathological liar and I want to be let down in every way. I want to give up all the dreams I ever had for myself in exchange for a few stale crumbs of false affection. I want to be kept on emotional tenterhooks, in constant mental turmoil as I wonder where I stand with him, what I'm doing wrong, how I can make him happy, where he really is right now and what will happen tomorrow. I want someone who will waste my time while he abuses me and diminishes me until I don't have the strength to stand up and walk away and I don't even want to. I want to learn to blame myself for all of this. And I want someone who can make me believe this is love."

Even though no one wants this for themselves, it is exactly what happens for many of us. How can this be? People are sucked into these relationships by way of charm and manipulation every day, and they are kept in them for many months or many years. Harm will result.

How does this happen, and what can you do about it?

Because of the incredible start the relationship got—the romance, the attraction, the mutual feeling of having found a soul mate—when things started taking one wrong turn after the next it will already be too late for you to walk away, if you went into the relationship without a clear picture of what you want and the determination to walk away when you find you're getting something very different.

That's why it is vital to know what you want before your next relationship begins. Then you'll have a chance of recognizing when you've become involved in something foul, because you'll see it's going off the course you charted. You will have a chance to see it for what it is before your self-worth becomes so damaged that you are willing to stay in a relationship where you have learned to accept being treated very poorly and not having your needs met (the needs to be loved, valued and respected are a few that come to mind).

What *are* your needs in a relationship, by the way? Make no mistake that your needs are every bit as important as everyone else's. If you don't believe that, you most likely have a people-pleasing mentality and are unconsciously asking to be disrespected and treated like a doormat. Not because you deserve it, of course, but because there are plenty of people who will take advantage of you.

We all have emotional needs; it's part of being human, and we should expect them to be fulfilled in our closest relationships. Our emotional needs include:

The need to be acknowledged.

The need to be accepted.

The need to be listened to.

The need to be understood.

The need to be loved.

The need to be appreciated.

The need to be respected.

The need to be valued.

The need to feel worthy.

The need to be trusted.

The need to feel capable and competent.

The need to feel clear (not confused).

The need to be supported.

The need to be safe, both physically and emotionally.

It's also vital to have a strong sense of self-worth and self-respect before your next potential partner comes along. If you don't, those who can sense that will be the ones who take an interest in you. This is a huge issue that far exceeds the scope of this blog post, yet it is contained within it in many ways.

How can you avoid becoming involved in a damaging relationship?

Start by doing some deep thinking and soul-searching, and decide on the details of the relationship you want in your life. Describe the other person's personality and traits. Describe how you'll feel in this relationship. Set clear boundaries, and be clear with yourself about why you have boundaries (to protect yourself; to find out a person's character by observing them over time and in different circumstances; to maintain your self-respect; to avoid wasting your time; etc.)

Boundaries include things such as, how much time will you spend with someone when you first meet? Will you maintain your current relationships and activities instead of dropping everything to spend every moment together? How long will you wait to have sex? What behavior is unacceptable to you?

When you can describe in detail the relationship you want in your life and the person you want to have it with and how you will feel in this relationship, and when you know what your boundaries are, you will be less likely to find yourself going along with whatever happens, less likely to get caught up in the other person's agenda without even realizing that you've given up your own.

When you define these things and make a commitment to yourself to honor them, you will then know that giving them up for someone—making concessions, bending the rules—is a red flag. Anyone who is truly interested in you and who is trustworthy will respect you for taking care of yourself and will not pressure you to move faster than you are ready to, nor will they walk away because of it.

Set your own agenda and stick with it, instead of becoming mindlessly caught up in someone else's.

12

FAITH THAT YOU WILL HEAL IS THE KEY TO HEALING

In your darkest hours, you may wonder if you will ever heal from something as awful as what you have been through, having been the victim of a psychopath. The experience might have left you questioning the meaning and purpose of your life, and of life in general. It may have shaken your belief in all you thought you knew about human nature, and left you feeling uncertain about everything, including yourself.

Where do you go from here?

There are some first steps that can get you started on the road that leads you up and out of the dark place you find yourself in now.

Gaining a clear understanding of what happened is necessary. It's important to have this understanding because when you do, you can begin to stop blaming yourself for the end of the relationship, and stop blaming yourself for having fallen for a predator and his or her manipulation.

You can start the process of regaining faith and trust in yourself by learning the details of how you were victimized. Doing so resolves shame, which is a roadblock that gets in the way of healing. Shame is the feeling of deep humiliation not for what we've done, but for what we are. No one should go through life with that belief about themselves.

Another vital part of the foundation of healing is faith. This doesn't mean religious faith (although that may be something that helps you, too); it refers to the belief that you will heal. Having faith that you will heal means that even after all you've been through, you want to heal and you believe that you will, even if at this point you don't have any idea how that will happen.

Faith that you will heal is a powerful first step. It's empowering to know that you simply need your own faith in order for the healing process to begin. It's really faith in yourself, and it is still within you even if you fear that you've lost it. Maybe it's been covered over by the psychopath's shovels full of dung, but it's there. Reclaim it as your own. This faith will grow into the determination and focus that will guide you through.

Even if you have no idea how healing is possible, it doesn't matter. You don't need to know to start the process.

Since we can't change the reality of what happened, regaining faith and trust in yourself should be your overarching goal. Psychopaths damage our self confidence, self respect and self worth, among other things. You can regain them, and even develop more than you had before.

From great adversity comes great strength. Just as the strongest steel is forged in the hottest fire, we too are forged and strengthened by the heat of our own struggles and triumphs.

In this moment, take a deep breath and feel the faith that you will heal, the faith that is the foundation for your healing.

13

HEALING IN THE AFTERMATH

You can heal after an victimization by a psychopath. It can take a significant amount of time and effort, as does any major trauma.

The illustration above shows Red Riding Hood being rescued from the Big Bad Wolf. I think it's safe to say that for most of us, this isn't going to happen. Once the "relationship" with the psychopath ends, we must rescue ourselves. Healing is something we must purposefully pursue.

We need the support of others after this trauma, but many of us find that support is hard to come by. Many people in our lives (friends, family, and even many therapists) don't understand psychopathy, so they may not understand the devastation we're experiencing. As a result, they're unable to give us the kind of support we need. Even we may not understand it at first. We just know we're devastated; we know something happened to us that was out of the ordinary, far beyond a relationship gone bad.

According to Dr. Robert Hare, "Virtually all of the research done in psychopathy is on the perpetrators, and we tend to ignore the tens of thousands of victims of these individuals. And most of the victims have nowhere to turn. They talk to their psychiatrist, psychologist, their friends, their employees, their priest, and they get nowhere because most people don't understand the nature of psychopathic people."

Since what we're dealing with is not the end of a regular relationship, no advice about healing after a breakup will help. We were victimized by predators who only pretended to establish a romantic relationship so they could manipulate and use us. But because it looked like a romantic relationship from the outside, it's hard for people to see beyond that. They don't understand the significant betrayal that took place or understand the trauma that causes. Even some victims don't see the truth, and are left believing they lost the love of their lives through some fault of their own.

None of us was "on the lookout for someone as brutal as a psychopath to systematically dismantle" the way we see ourselves, as author Sandra L. Brown, M.A., wrote in her book, *The Unexamined Victim: Women Who Love Psychopaths.* We never expected the person who claimed to love us was really out to destroy our self-worth through cruel and methodical emotional manipulation. No wonder victims don't get the support they need; this scenario simply isn't comprehensible to those who haven't experienced it.

One thing a victim needs is validation. Brown says "It is pathology websites, books and programs that help women heal when they find their validation in other stories, research, books, forums, and organizations designed to respond to pathological love relationships.

The validation you are seeking comes from others who have been through it," writes Brown's in her article, "Recovering Without Validation" published on the *Psychology Today* website.

Although online forums can be helpful, a word of warning is necessary.

In the search for support and validation, many join online forums. Be very cautious if you are newly traumatized. There is the potential for secondary victimization that goes on, sometimes the work of trolls, or other survivors who may mean well, but who spread erroneous and sometimes harmful ideas that perpetuate victim-blaming. Even so, many people do have positive experiences in forums. There is tremendous value in speaking with other survivors. There is just as much potential for harm as there is for help, though. Some have experienced abuse and suffered more trauma while participating in a forum (I was one of them). Please keep this in mind and be very cautious. If something doesn't feel right, listen to that feeling. Part of healing is learning to trust your perceptions.

After going through such a severe trauma, help is necessary, and there is help and support for you out there but you need to be determined to find it. Recovery is an active process that you need to take part in. In doing so, you demonstrate to yourself that you believe in your own worth and you have faith that you will heal.

Challenges for the victim of a psychopath include:

- Finding help and support;

- Recovering from harm to your psyche, heart and soul; including self-blame, shame, betrayal, anger, doubt, fear, moral injury, grief, and uncertainty or groundlessness;

- Dealing with challenges to your ability to trust others and yourself;

- Breaking the 'betrayal bond' that keeps victims emotionally attached to their abuser;

- Feeling pressure to forgive the perpetrator;

- Experiencing cognitive dissonance, a key element that can stand in the way of healing, which I'll talk about next;

and

- Not only dealing with recovery from serious trauma, but also dealing with grief over the loss of the person you loved. This piece of the puzzle is often neglected or diminished because the psychopath only pretended to love, but it is another important key to healing. Remember, the psychopath established an intense relationship during the idealization phase; without that, the manipulation and abuse could never have happened. While it's true the man or woman you loved never really existed, your love for him or her was real, and that love deserves and needs your acknowledgement, approval and compassion before you can let it go.

That is a lot to deal with.

Books and websites are helpful, and by all means you should read and learn as much as you can. There are many resources listed on my website, Psychopaths and Love. But they may not be enough to help you overcome the trauma you've experienced.

It's important to see a psychotherapist (psychologist or social worker) who specializes in psychological trauma and abusive relationships, if at all possible.

As a result of the trauma, you may be suffering from depression, a stress disorder or PTSD (post traumatic stress disorder), major depression, panic disorder or an anxiety disorder.

You're probably struggling with difficult or even unbearable emotions, disturbing memories, intrusive thoughts and a sense of constant danger.

Many victims describe being unable to trust, feeling extremely vulnerable, experiencing rage, having obsessive thoughts, and experiencing fear and anxiety. Their self-esteem and self-confidence are low.

Some turn to alcohol or drugs or develop a physical illness, or experience irrational and extreme behavior such as total isolation and withdrawal. Some will contemplate suicide.

Symptoms are sometimes so severe that victims are incorrectly diagnosed as paranoid, delusional, or as having borderline personality disorder.

The aftermath of emotional trauma needs to be taken seriously. That's why you should make every effort to see a mental health professional who is a trauma expert if you need it.

You may also want to look into a support group for abuse victims, run by a mental health professional. Your local domestic violence center probably has such a group.

If you are feeling suicidal, please don't try to deal with it alone. There are people who will listen to you, without judgment. I hope you will call a suicide prevention hotline immediately if you are feeling this way.

You will heal eventually. Many of us have, and you will become one of us. You are not alone.

14

YOUR OWN PERSONAL APOCALYPSE

"I can't go on. I'll go on."
Samuel Beckett

Most of us have said those words in the aftermath. At first, we think "I can't go on." Those days are the darkest.

At some point, we dare to think "I'll go on," even though we're not sure how. We can see beyond the end of the world, but we're not sure what we will find or how we will get there.

We are standing amidst the rubble of our own personal apocalypse.

Hopes, dreams, plans and promises lay strewn about in unsalvageable tatters. Time evaporates along with them, months and years were lost forever beneath the ruins.

Worst of all, our trust in others and in ourselves is reduced to charred and smoldering bits, along with our beliefs about life and the world. Our lives were changed beyond recognition by a force outside our knowledge and comprehension. Even worse, that force was someone we thought we knew, someone we loved and trusted. Only fear and pain remained, unscathed.

Those who haven't experienced a psychopath would read what I've written so far and say I am being overly dramatic. Those of us who have, know that what I've written so far is an accurate description.

But we do go on. We develop resilience and we find strength we never knew we had. After making your long and difficult journey, what will you find in that place beyond the end of your world?

That is entirely up to you.

Many people go through life without experiencing something so destructive that it blows their entire world to bits. They can hold on to the things that get them by and live a pretty benign day-to-day existence, same as it ever was. There's nothing wrong with that.

But we don't have that option anymore.

Many things have been buried under the rubble, but even more have been revealed. Things are different now. We see things you didn't see before. Our rose-colored glasses are off, smashed somewhere amidst the ruins, and our eyes are opened to a clearer vision of reality. Each new insight leads to another.

When you heal, you may find you don't tolerate time-wasting games anymore, from others or from yourself. You may find that you can easily spot those now. You may find that you aren't so easily upset, angered or frustrated as you were in the past. You may find that you appreciate the good things more, and the simple things. The real things. You may find that you now have a lot more room for these things in your life, since everything else was obliterated. You may find that you are very picky about who and what you let into your new world.

You will go on. The question is, what will you go on to? What life will you create after your long journey to beyond the end of the world?

Under the rocks and stones, there is water flowing.

15

TRAITS OF THE PSYCHOPATH'S VICTIM

Are there certain traits that make us vulnerable to psychopathic victimization?

There are, but this in no way suggests a victim is to blame—the predator is clearly the one to blame. Everyone has vulnerabilities, and that's only a problem because there are those who will exploit them.

These traits apply to both men and women. As you read them, you'll probably find you have several. It's important to know what yours are, so you can be alert for someone who is zeroing in on them.

Traits of the psychopath's victim:

- A general demeanor of vulnerability, which the psychopath can easily detect. Vulnerability can come from many things:

- Not having gotten love, support or validation from your family of origin

- Isolation from friends and family

- Loss of a job

- Being new in town

- Longing for a relationship

- A strong need for attention, approval or support

- A previous victimization that is unresolved

- Illness

- Long-term stress

- Loss of a loved one through death, divorce or a breakup

- Weak or unclear personal boundaries

- Boredom. When you're bored, you have the desire for excitement. A brand new relationship can relieve boredom quickly — especially one with a psychopath.

- Loneliness. If you're lonely, your unmet social and emotional needs create an opening for a psychopath to enter your life. You're probably also bored, which elevates risk. You may have gotten used to feeling like this, so it just seems like life as usual. But a psychopath — who is very adept at reading people — will recognize it for what it is, and take advantage of it.

- The desire for a relationship

We're all vulnerable at times, and there's nothing wrong with that. But during these times that we need to pay special attention to who is giving us attention. Some periods of vulnerability can be extended, such as when you're single and desiring a relationship; or they can be ongoing, if you have a chronic sense of low self-worth.

It's sad but true—the psychopath will hit you when you're down, although he'll act like he's appeared in your life as the perfect person to fulfill your needs and desires. Vulnerable people are the easiest to victimize, and the psychopath can bond with them quickly and deeply with promises of providing something they desperately want.

"The callous use of the lonely is a trademark of psychopaths."

Dr. Robert Hare

Stressful life events create a general demeanor of vulnerability—which the psychopath sees as weakness and neediness—that reveals itself through mannerisms and subtle signals conveyed by the way you walk, your posture, your facial expressions, the amount of eye contact you make, and the tone of your voice.

What can you do?

When you're going through any kind of hard time in life, when you have some deep need that is unfulfilled, when you're lonely or when you're experiencing anything on the list above, be aware that you're giving off vibes of vulnerability and be wary of new people who enter your life, especially those who seem offer a solution to your problem or an answer to your prayer. Especially if they seem too good to be true.

According to Dr. Hare, psychopaths indirectly communicate four basic things to seduce their victims:

I like who you are.

I'm just like you.

Your secrets are safe with me.

I'm the perfect partner for you.

To the vulnerable person the psychopath seems to be *exactly* what they need, so they happily take the bait. They believe their deepest desires have been fulfilled and their problems have been solved.

Actually, their problems are just beginning.

Psychopaths have a relentless need for self-gratification. They know exactly what your needs are, and they have the ability to put on whatever mask (persona) is necessary to get what they want from you. The psychopath gives you a delicious taste of what it is you need, which gives him or her great power over you. The realization that they could also take it away gives them even more power, and they play that hand for all it's worth.

Having needs is normal. For example, as humans we need love. That only becomes a problem when we believe there is only one person who can fulfill that need, one perfect partner who seems like our soul mate, who seems to know exactly what we lack and who seems to provide it so well. That's the hook, the line and the sinker. It's also untrue, but the victim can't see this when caught up close and personal in the psychopath's sticky web of deceit. After the fact, you'll realize there was absolutely no substance to it; you'll see the love the psychopath claimed to feel for you was like a mirage. In the desert, a mirage appears from a distance as a shimmering pool of water, but upon closer investigation you'll find there's not one drop to quench your thirst. It only looked that way.

Psychopaths see human traits that they don't have (love, insecurity, trust, compassion, fear) as weaknesses to exploit. They feel they have a right to victimize vulnerable people because they see them as weak or even worthless. They gain your trust and love only to gain control over you to get what they want.

If you aren't aware your own deepest fears, desires, motivations and needs (and many people aren't), you leave yourself open to the control of a manipulator. By knowing your own vulnerabilities, you can become aware of possible attempts at exploitation. Awareness of your "weak spots" gives you a chance to thwart an attack.

When someone knows you better than you know yourself, you're at great risk. Take the time now to learn your vulnerabilities; it can help you to prevent victimization. Know yourself well, which means knowing all the places where you're needy, lacking, wounded, fearful, or otherwise vulnerable.

Even traits we normally think of as positive can be used against us by a psychopath:

- Are you extroverted? This can increase your risk, because extroverted people are easily bored and generally curious, and are usually looking for excitement.

- Do you "go with the flow?" This trait could make you more willing to accept the chaos a psychopath creates in your life.

- Are you competitive? Then you're better able to deal with a psychopath's dominant personality. You're also more likely to stubbornly hold on when it seems the psychopath is doing all he can to get you to end the relationship.

- Are you sentimental? Then you may be more likely to focus on the good memories of a relationship instead of the bad ones.

- Are you sensitive to other people's feelings? You probably care a lot about what others think of you, and tend to put their feelings ahead of your own.

- Are you relaxed and carefree? Then you may not see danger in a person or situation as readily as a cautious person might.

Other traits that will put you at risk:

- Being overly trusting,

- Being very loyal

- Being committed to helping others reach their potential.

Notice that all of us are described on these lists. Most people are at risk, whether they think so or not.

Awareness of the vulnerabilities and traits that put you at risk is an important part of preventing involvement with a psychopath. To learn more about these and other traits, read the book by Sandra Brown, M.A., *"Women Who Love Psychopaths."*

"Know yourself. Psychopaths are skilled at detecting and ruthlessly exploiting your weak spots. Your best defense is to understand what these spots are, and to be extremely wary of anyone who zeroes in on them." writes Dr. R. Hare, in the article "How to Spot Social Predators Before They Attack"

When the perfect person comes along and fulfills your wishes like a genie from a magic lamp, look closely for the substance behind it and look closely at the true character of the genie. It's hard to think critically and look for problems when you believe you've found someone who gives you just what you need, but it is necessary.

16

THE SELF-COMPASSION EFFECT

"A moment of self-compassion can change your entire day. A string of such moments can change the course of your life."

Christopher K. Germer

Step outside yourself for a moment, if you will, and take a look.

There you are, the 'you' who was mistreated and who is now treating yourself so harshly, who is feeling shame, despair, doubt, outrage, confusion, self-doubt, deep sadness, anger, self-judgment or rage. What a sad thing for this 'you' to go through! This loving and giving you does not deserve this pain. It is truly heartbreaking to behold.

Empathy makes your heart overflow, and you have the desire to provide comfort. You look softly and with kindness upon this you who is mourning the loss or raging at injustice or betrayal, and you place a warm hand gently on a shoulder that shakes with sobs. You feel completely accepting of the intense emotions this you is experiencing. You tell this you that whatever feelings he or she is experiencing are OK. You know this is how a loving human heart feels when it breaks. You care deeply about this you and want to help you deal with this trauma.

What you're feeling is self-compassion.

"Self-compassion means truly honoring, and allowing for, our own suffering. To be with the hurt, the longing, and the hunger, and to offer value and substance to these experiences. More than that, to go further and to respond, in kind, to what the self is really wanting and needing," writes Lisa Field-Elliott.

According to Buddhanet, Compassion is made up of two words: 'co' meaning together and 'passion' meaning a strong feeling. This is what compassion is. When we see someone is in distress and we feel their pain as if it were our own, and strive to eliminate or lessen their pain, then this is compassion. "So all the best in human beings, all the qualities like sharing, readiness to give comfort, sympathy, concern and caring—all are manifestations of compassion. You will notice also that in the compassionate person, care and love towards others has its origins in care and love for oneself."

Compassion often involves an empathic response and an altruistic behavior. However, compassion is defined as the emotional response when perceiving suffering and involves an authentic desire to help.

> "Who will you love if not yourself? Other people? How can you love someone for anything but their raw, naked humanity? How can you say you love someone if it is not for their flaws and quirks, snorts and hurts, triggers and tears? Anything else is not love. It is idealization. And, as long as you do it to yourself, you will do it to everyone. You will not love anyone or anything until those eyes in the mirror soften up and embrace the beauty that is already within."
>
> Vironika Tugaleva

You didn't feel any compassion from the psychopath, who was callous and cold-hearted. After it was over you may not have felt it from friends or family members who didn't understand your experience. You may not have felt it from yourself as you judged yourself harshly for falling for manipulation, or for not seeing it sooner, or for staying too long. You go looking for support, kindness, understanding, validation and assistance. You have an innate need for compassion.

The cure for a lack of compassion is compassion.

The components of compassion—recognition of hurt, suffering, and injustice; tenderheartedness toward, and a desire to alleviate distress—take a powerful stance against past wrongs and champion healing. This makes compassion diametrically opposed to callousness, indifference and heartlessness.

Whether you find compassion in others or not (and I sincerely hope you do), you can become compassionate toward yourself. It's more important now than ever, but cultivating self-compassion will serve you well all your life. Self-compassion is transformational after a trauma such as ours. And it has proven benefits:

"Research shows that people who practice self-compassion have better mental health, less anxiety and depression, and are just as successful at meeting goals as those who don't. One longer-term study showed that self-compassion helped people to adjust better, after a divorce. When we get disappointed in life, our natural tendency might be to ask ourselves what we did wrong, but saying to ourselves, 'You did the best you could given what you knew at the time,' can help us to feel better about ourselves and give us courage to begin rebuilding our lives," writes Melanie Greenberg, Ph.D, in "Why Self-Compassion Helps You Meet Life's Challenges."

There are three core components to self-compassion, according to Kristen Neff, leading self-compassion researcher and educator:

"The first one is self-kindness, as opposed to self-judgment. A lot of times when we suffer, we just take a very cold attitude toward ourselves. So self-compassion involves being warm and supportive—actively soothing ourselves—as opposed to being cold and judging ourselves.

The second part is remembering that imperfection is part of the shared human experience—that you're not alone in your suffering. Often, when something goes wrong, we look in the mirror and don't like what we see—we feel very isolated in that moment, as if everyone else has these perfect lives and it's just us who's flawed and defective. When we remember that imperfection is part of the shared human experience, you can actually feel more connected to people in those moments.

The third component is mindfulness. If you aren't mindfully aware that you're suffering, if you're just repressing your pain or ignoring it or getting lost in problem solving, you can't give yourself compassion. You have to say, 'Wait a second. This hurts. This is really hard. This is a moment where I need compassion.' If you don't want to go there, if it's too painful or you're just too busy to go there, you can't be compassionate."

Being victimized by a psychopath is something we never anticipated, and not something everyone experiences. It's not a trauma we ever expected to go through in life, and it is a major one. This trauma comes with a sense of being cut off from normal life and from the rest of humanity. But part of self-compassion entails feeling a sense of common humanity, which is the understanding that your feelings and experiences are not completely unique. By acknowledging we're not the only one, we find strength in numbers.

Even those of us who've gone through this bizarre experience of psychopathic victimization are not alone.

"In reality, sadly, part of humanity is humans doing terrible things to other humans, including children. Survivors do not need to travel anywhere or change ourselves to rejoin the human race. We are already right here," writes Sonia Connelly, in "From Shame to Compassion: Reconciling with Ourselves after Abuse."

There is an important difference between self-compassion and self-esteem. Self-compassion isn't based on self-judgment, comparison and outcomes, as self-esteem is. Self-esteem is about being above average, but self-compassion is all about being average. It's about being human (which is something to celebrate after being with a psychopath) and being a part of the shared human condition. We all have successes and failures and strengths and weaknesses. Self-compassion acknowledges and accepts all of them.

"Acceptance of one's life has nothing to do with resignation; it does not mean running away from the struggle. On the contrary, it means accepting it as it comes, with all the handicaps of heredity, of suffering, of psychological complexes and injustices."

Paul Tournier

Self-compassion is nothing less than a paradigm shift after involvement with a psychopath. It can be transformational. Being human becomes OK again (psychopaths despise that) along with all the emotions we feel, which are, after all, universal. Compassion is healing; it's a treatment for the harm suffered from being treated without compassion.

Under all the lies abusers pile on us is our true and original self, intact—a unique being with innate value whose life has meaning and worth, who is meant to give and receive love through meaningful connections with others and with ourselves. That's definitely worth having compassion for. You are definitely worth having compassion for.

"It's simply being kind to myself—meeting myself, whatever my emotional, physical or psychological state, with loving kindness. As simple, and difficult, as that!"

Marianne Elliott

17

FEELINGS OF LOSS AND GRIEF AFTER THE PSYCHOPATH IS GONE?

"Only people who are capable of loving strongly can also suffer great sorrow."
Leo Tolstoy

A reader named Joanna left a comment on my website that said, "I hate myself for missing him. Now I'm grieving badly and I so want to get rid of this heartache and heal."

No matter if you end the relationship or the psychopath discards you, there will be some rough times ahead. That's not surprising since you are going through a serious trauma. Part of that trauma—and one that takes some victims by surprise—are feelings of profound loss and deep grief. This may not happen right away. But as things start to resolve and it becomes more quiet inside, grief is often what's left standing, waiting for your attention.

This aspect of the trauma seems perplexing. These uncomfortable feelings of loss are often denied, neglected or diminished by the victim, her friends and family, and even her counselor if she has one. After all, you just went through months or years of victimization by a man or woman who never loved you in the first place. How could you be grieving over such an unhealthy relationship with someone who was so terrible? Feelings of guilt and shame set in. But the grief is still there, waiting.

Remember, the psychopath established an intense bond with you during the idealization phase; without that, the manipulation and abuse could never have happened. You may have believed this person was the love of your life. Trying to hold on to that, and seeming to recapture it from time to time, is what made it all possible. Now, the part of you that believed and hoped and dreamed has finally realized there is nothing to try to hold on to anymore, and your feelings of loss can be profound.

Even if it's true that the person you loved wasn't who you thought he or she was and the relationship wasn't what you believed it to be, your love was real and so is your loss. Your love and loss deserve and need your acknowledgement, acceptance, compassion and grief. Grieving is necessary for healing.

Unresolved grief can leave emotional scars and depression behind. An understanding therapist can be very helpful in this situation if family and friends aren't able to be there for you in an accepting and non-judgmental way (or if you're not able to be there for yourself in an accepting and non-judgmental way).

The loss we face is experienced by many as being the same as a death. The person we loved is gone, and is not coming back. Unfortunately, many of us experience what is known as disenfranchised grief. If one is disenfranchised they are deprived a right to something. Because of society's rules our situation is not seen as worthy of grief, and therefore not worthy of the support one would usually extend at such a time. The relationship was abusive, and many believe it is not appropriate to grieve over the loss of an abusive partner. Our grief is invalidated. As a result, we question our own feelings. We may try to "get over it" or we stop talking about it to others. We believe our feelings are wrong, and we feel alone.

While you may not get the support we need from others, you don't have to deny your grief. Your feelings of loss exist for good reason and deserve and need your acknowledgement, acceptance and compassion. Explore and express your emotions. Your love was real and valid, and so is your grief.

18

HOW TO HELP A FRIEND WHO WAS VICTIMIZED BY A PSYCHOPATH

"We shall be friends to those heartbroken and in sorrow. We shall share their sorrow."

Rumi

When victims reach out to their family and friends after being victimized by a psychopath, many are disappointed by their responses. Deeply disappointed. A victim may have spent months or even years with someone who had no ability to feel love or empathy, and the last thing they need are loved ones who are unsupportive and invalidating.

People who haven't had the experience of being traumatized by a psychopath simply can't understand it. But they can see that their friend needs support, and support can be offered regardless of whether they understand what happened or not. Unfortunately, support sometimes is tied to understanding, so responses may lack genuineness and originality. Friends and family may offer platitudes and cliches which aren't helpful and can even be hurtful to the victim. Here's an example, These words were spoken to me by a friend:

> "Why continue to waste precious energy? Why would you give him that satisfaction? It seems to me that you are responsible to yourself for releasing him from your life."

To a victim, words like these are completely meaningless, empty and cold-hearted, and lacking in kindness and empathy. They invalidate the victim's trauma by suggesting he or she just forgets about it, just somehow lets it go, as if that should be an easy thing for them to do.

Our culture has been so permeated by new-age and pop-psychology junk that invalidation has unfortunately become the norm. Many people can't think of original things to say during a crisis. Someone hears something, and *ding!* a new-age pop-psych platitude pops out of their mouth without any thought or care behind it, just like a Pop Tart pops out of a toaster, mechanically and devoid of any nourishment. Empty calories, empty words. Junk food for the soul.

So how do you help a friend who was victimized by a psychopath or anyone else going through any hard time in their life? By having empathy. Judging someone's feelings, and then finding them to be invalidate and then withholding support, is the opposite of empathy.

Empathy is the ability to be aware of another person's thoughts and feelings, and having the wherewithal to express this awareness. It also means creating mutual understanding and a sense of caring for one another. It's not empathy unless you respond appropriately to the other person.

> "One doesn't have to operate with great malice to do great harm. The absence of empathy and understanding are sufficient."
>
> Charles M. Blow

How can you show empathy for a friend in the aftermath?

First, listen to them, without judgement. Really listen, without thinking of what you're going to say next. And not just to their words, but to the emotions they're expressing.

Resist the temptation to utter anything that's not completely original, such as any type of empty, meaningless (and often heartless) platitude. Tell them that you understand they're suffering and that you're sorry. If it comes from your heart, it will be very comforting.

Make an attempt to understand what they've been through. Ask questions, and let them talk about their experience. Even if you can't understand what they've experienced, surely as a friend you can at least connect with the fact that they're in pain and need your support and kindness.

Ask your friend what you can do to support them, and then do it.

Check on your friend daily, even if they tell you they're OK.

If your friend is not functioning or is suicidal, find help for them.

And keep these words in mind:

> "The friend who can be silent with us in a moment of despair or confusion, who can stay with us in an hour of grief and bereavement, who can tolerate not knowing, not curing, not healing, and face with us the reality of our powerlessness, that is a friend who cares."
>
> Henri Nouwen

You don't need to come up with the perfect thing to say or with the solutions to their problem. Your silent, caring presence can ease the pain more than you could ever imagine.

To learn what NOT to say, I will turn to an article on "new-age bullies" written by Julia Ingram:

"I call them New Age Bullies—those who, sometimes with the best intentions, repeat spiritual movement shibboleths, with little understanding of how hurtful their advice can be. Some of their favorite clichés are:

It happened for a reason.

Nobody can hurt you without your consent.

I wonder why you created this illness (or experience).

There are no accidents.

There are no victims.

There are no mistakes.

A variant of this behavior is found in the self-bullying people who blame themselves for being victims of a crime, accident, or illness and interpret such misfortunes as evidence of their personal defects or spiritual deficiencies."

Many relationships do not survive because of the invalidation and lack of empathy shown to the victim. According to Steve Hein, MSW, "Rejecting feelings is rejecting reality; it is to fight nature and may be called a crime against nature, 'psychological murder' or 'soul murder.' Considering that trying to fight feelings, rather than accept them, is trying to fight all of nature, you can see why it is so frustrating, draining and futile."

So what types of things should you say?

The following statements convey validation and empathy:

That must have been hard.

I hear you.

That's not good.

That's a lot to deal with.

I would feel the same way.

That's sad.

That must really hurt.

I would feel the same way.

I can understand how you feel.

It sounds like you are really feeling _____.

I can see that you are really upset.

You look very sad.

Would you like to talk about it?

That really bothered you, didn't it.

What bothers you the most about it?

What would help you feel better?

What can I do to help you?

In contrast, invalidation communicates that a person's emotions, thoughts and perceptions are not valid—they are unwarranted, irrational, overblown, selfish, stupid or wrong. Invalidation is the last thing your friend needs. He or she got plenty of it from the psychopath.

When a friend is traumatized, make communication meaningful by choosing compassionate, validating words that come from your heart.

19

FREEDOM FROM THE PSYCHOPATH

All things human hang by a slender thread; and that which seemed to stand strong suddenly falls and sinks in ruins

Ovid

The illusion of the psychopath "standing strong" can't last. Cracks appear in his mask of smoke and mirrors. One day, the psychopath will no longer have any power over you. He will "fall and sink in ruins" when you realize he never really stood strong, that it was all deception. That will be hard to accept, but with acceptance comes freedom.

ABOUT THE AUTHOR

Adelyn Birch is the author of the website Psychopaths and Love. She was victimized by a psychopath. She reaches out to others who have been traumatized in this way, in an effort to share what she's learned and to offer validation, encouragement and support.

OTHER BOOKS BY THE AUTHOR:

Boundaries: Loving Again After a Pathological Relationship

MORE Psychopaths and Love (A collection of essays to inspire healing and empowerment)

30 Covert Emotional Manipulation Tactics

202 Ways to Spot a Psychopath in Personal Relationships